WorkBook

Alphabet

Alligator and apple

Trace and print **A** and **a**.

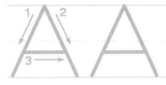

The word **acorn** starts with **Aa**.
Trace the word.

acorn

Look up, down, and across. Find
the word **ANT** 6 times in the puzzle.

B A L L G
A N T A O
T T O N A
C A N T N
A N T U T

Bb

Trace and print **B** and **b**.

Butterfly starts with the letter **Bb**. Count the butterflies, then draw your own.

How many?

Cc

Cow and calf

Trace and print **C** and **c**.

The word **carrot** starts with **Cc**.
Trace the word.

carrot

Circle the things that start with **c**.

can

cat

corn

snail

Dd

Dinosaur and donut

Trace and print **D** and **d**.

D D

d d

Circle each animal that has the letter **d** in its name.

dog

cow

dolphin

lizard

lion

wildebeest

E e

Eagle and eggs

Trace and print **E** and **e**.

The word **elephant** starts with **Ee**.
Trace the word.

elephant

Finish the **Ee** patterns.
What comes next?

1 E e E ☐

2 E E E ☐

3 e E E ☐

4 e e e ☐

F f

Trace and print **F** and **f**.

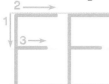

Fish starts with **Ff**.
Count the fish,
then draw more
of your own.

How many
in all?

G g

Gorilla and guitar

Trace and print **G** and **g**.

G G

g g

Circle the things that start with the letter **g**.

grapes

giraffe

popcorn

The word **gerbil** starts with **Gg**. Trace the word.

gerbil

Hh

ha-ha!!!

Hyena and helmet

Trace and print **H** and **h**.

The word **honey** starts with **Hh**.
Trace the word.

honey

Count the **H**'s and the **h**'s.

h	H	H	h	H
h	h	H	h	h
H	h	H	H	H
h	h	H	H	H

How many **H**'s?

How many **h**'s?

I i

Trace and print **I** and **i**.

Ice cube starts with **Ii**.

Draw more **ice cubes** to complete an **igloo**.

J j

Jaguar and jam

Trace and print **J** and **j**.

Circle the things that start with the letter **j**.

juice

balloon

jet

A baby kangaroo is called a **joey**. Trace the word.

joey

Kk

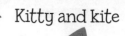
Kitty and kite

Trace and print **K** and **k**.

K K

k k

Create a colorful **kite**.

The word **kiwi** starts with **Kk**.
Trace the word.

kiwi

L l

Lion and lamp

Trace and print **L** and **l**.

Leaf starts with **Ll**.
Color the **leaves**.

Mm

Trace and print **M** and **m**.

M M M

m m m

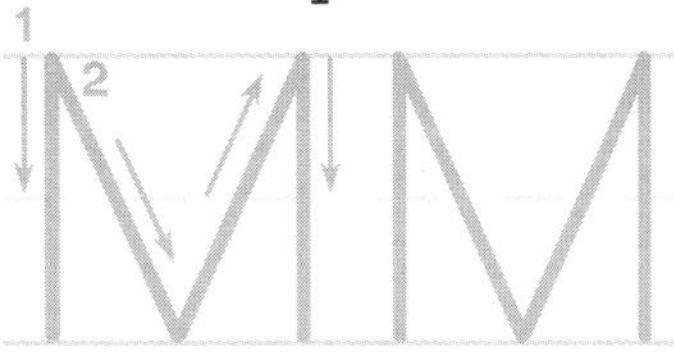

Circle the things that start with the letter **m**.

moths

sun

tree

rock

mushrooms

swing

N n

Narwhal and net

Trace and print **N** and **n**.

Follow each **N** to the end of the maze.

start

N	N	V	V	V	V
N	P	T	C	G	G
N	N	T	C	Y	G
S	N	T	O	Y	Y
S	N	N	O	N	N
S	S	N	N	N	N

finish

Circle the things that start with the letter **n**.

nail

nest

nut

worm

Octopus and orange

Trace and print **O** and **o**.

Orange starts with **Oo**.
Circle the things that have
the color orange.

giraffe

parrot

grapes

dinosaur

apple

fox

P p

Pirate and painting

Trace and print **P** and **p**.

P P

p p

The word **penguin** starts with **Pp**.
Trace the word.

penguin

Color the **pansies pink** and **purple**.

Qq

Trace and print **Q** and **q**.

Q Q Q

q q q

The word **queen** starts with **Qq**. Trace the word, then design a crown fit for a **queen**!

queen

Create a colorful **quilt**.

Rr

Rainbow and rabbit

Trace and print **R** and **r**.

R R

r r

Red starts with **Rr**.
Circle the things that have some red.

cat

fire truck

radish

corn

hot dog

dog

robot

Ss

Trace and print **S** and **s**.

S S

S S

The word **square** starts with **Ss**. Color each square.

Follow each letter **S** to the end of the maze.

start

S	S	S	B	B	F
S	S	S	B	B	F
S	R	K	K	K	F
S	R	K	K	F	F
S	R	S	S	S	A
S	S	S	S	S	A

finish

T t

Trace and print **T** and **t**.

Trumpet starts with **Tt**.
Circle the things that start with the letter **t**.

truck

trumpet

bed

cheese

tree

toucan

gloves

crab

U u

Unicorn and umbrella

Trace and print **U** and **u**.

Urchin starts with **Uu**.
Circle and count the urchins.

How many?

V v

Trace and print **V** and **v**.

Circle the images that start with the letter **v**.

mushroom

volleyball

vase

van

Decorate and color the **Valentine**.

 Ww

Trace and print **W** and **w**.

Worm starts with **Ww**.
Circle and count the worms.

How many? ☐

X-ray and xylophone

Trace and print **X** and **x**.

X-ray fish starts with **Xx**.
Cross out the things that **don't** have the letter **x** in their names.

fox

X-ray fish

ladybug

six

burger

box

kiwifruit

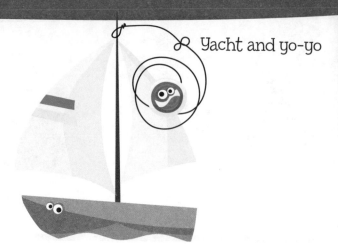

Yacht and yo-yo

Trace and print **Y** and **y**.

Yellow starts with the letter **Yy**.
Color the stars yellow.

Circle the things that have the letter **y** in their names.

yak

basketball

bicycle

Z z

Zebra and zucchini

Trace and print **Z** and **z**.

1 → Z Z

1 → z z

Circle the things that start with the letter **z**.

zero

zipper

sunglasses

basket

fries

camel

zigzag

Draw lines to match the letter pairs.

A B C D E

b d a e c

F G H I J

i j f g h

J

K L M N O

m o l k n

Draw lines to match the letter pairs.

P Q R S T U

t s p q u r

V W X Y Z

w z y v x

B D P Q G

p g b d q

Color the alphabet of objects!

A   B   C   D

E   F   G   H

I   J   K   L

M   N   O

P

Q

R

S

T

U

V

W

X

Y

Z

Practice printing the alphabet.

A B C D E F G H I J K L M N O P Q R S T U V W X Y Z
a b c d e f g h i j k l m n o p q r s t u v w x y z